Jack and Billy

Story by Jenny Giles

Illustrations by Betty Greenhatch

"Here is my car,"

said Jack.

"Brrrm, brrrm,"

said Jack.

"Here I come in my car."

"Look at my car," said Jack.

8

"Come in my car, Billy,"

said Jack.

"No," said Billy.

"Come here, Billy,"

said Jack.

"Look!"

"Look at my car,"

said Billy.

"Brrrm, brrrm," said Billy.

"Here I come in **my** car."